let's travel in the

CONGO

By Glenn D. Kittler

Edited by Darlene Geis

A TRAVEL PRESS BOOK

SECOND PRINTING

PICTURE ACKNOWLEDGMENTS

The color illustrations in this book are the work of the following photographers and artists, whose collaboration is gratefully acknowledged. For the full-color pictures Patellani, from P.I.P. Photos (1, 2, 4, 5, 7, 10, 12, 13, 14, 15, 17, 18, 20, 21, 22, 23, 24, 25, 26, 28, 29, 30, 31, 32); David Shapiro (3); Ed Gallob, from Rapho-Guillumette (6, 8); and Paul D. Smith, Africafilms (9, 11, 16, 19, 27). For the black-and-white photographs we wish to thank Paul D. Smith, Africafilms; The Bettmann Archive; Associated Press; Wide World Photos; the Belgian Government Information Center; and The Museum of Primitive Art of New York. The map was made by Enrico Arno.

Library of Congress Catalog Card Number: 65-28200

CONTENTS

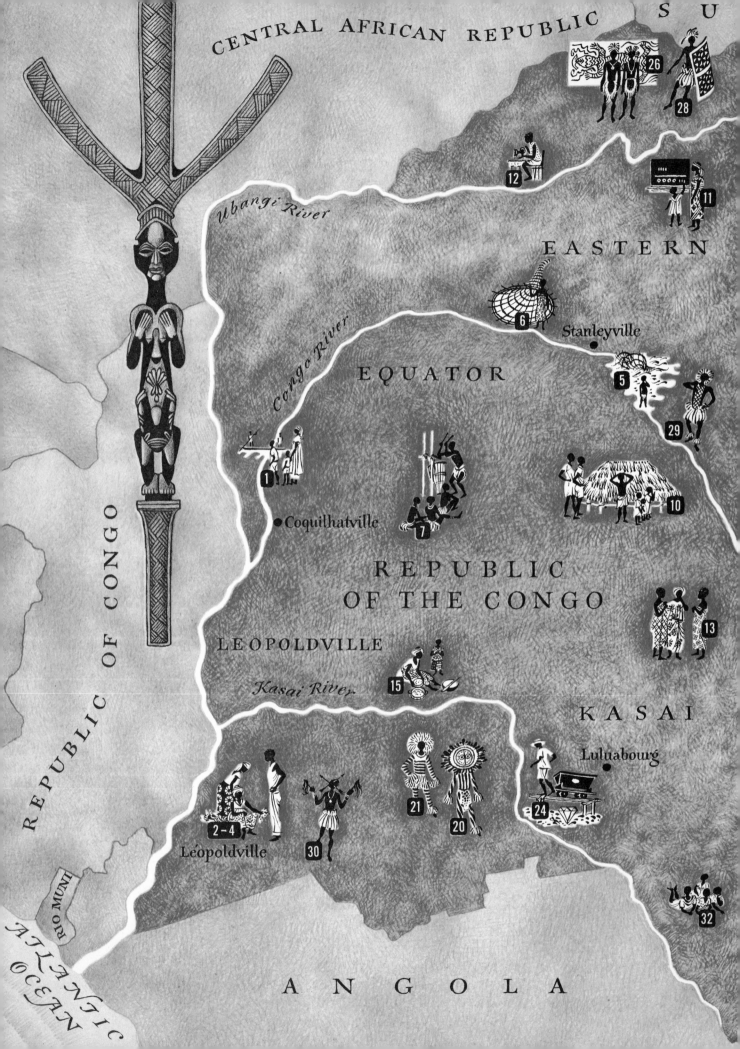

Locales of thirty-two full-page pictures

THE CONGO,

HEART OF AFRICA

THE Congo reaches out at you. Flying south from the Mediterranean, you still have an hour to travel when you perceive the sudden thickening of forests that foretells your approach to the land that has been called "the Heart of Darkness." Or if your plane comes in over the Atlantic you are still far out at sea when you behold the dark-brown waters of the Congo River, spilling their burden of silt into the blue ocean. Even before you set foot in the country, you are aware that you are entering a world of dramatic differences, a Janus world with one face gazing backward over centuries of primitive life, the other face looking ahead to a future rich with promise.

The Republic of the Congo was born on the 30th of June, 1960, when Belgium granted independence to the country that had been known for half a century as the Belgian Congo. Shaped like a giant bowl, with highlands and mountains surrounding a low plateau, the Congo is the basin of the mighty Congo River. It lies almost at the center of Africa with a small lip extending to the Atlantic coast, where the river pours into the sea.

"Congo" is an African word that means rain forest, and almost half of this country—the northeast, and the central portion, through which the equator cuts—is steamy and wet, with dense stands of enormous trees. The sun scarcely filters through the thick foliage, and in the dim light of the forest floor, dark hunters and soft-footed animals move swiftly and silently.

But there is more to the Congo than equatorial forests and jungles. This enormous country is 900,000 square miles in area—almost as large as India or the third of the United States that reaches from the Mississippi to the Atlantic Ocean. Yet this vast country, whose mineral wealth is still not fully developed, has a population of only 13,000,000 people as compared with India's teeming 350,000,000.

Within the far-reaching borders of the Congo is a world of paradox, immune to time. The uranium that went into the first atom bomb was dug out of Congo hills by men who still hunt with spears. Most of the mine workers in the Katanga (*kah-*TAHNG-*gah*) Province copper fields migrate to their jobs in airplanes, but few of them have ever been inside

9

an automobile. The Congo produces over 70 per cent of the world's industrial diamonds in Kasai (*kah*-SIGH) Province, yet the most prized Congolese adornment is a leopard's tooth.

A visitor to the Congo can walk out of his air-conditioned hotel room and ten minutes later photograph a witch doctor removing a curse from a terrified man. He can have a lunch of stewed bananas and lima beans in a mud hut, then ten minutes later drink the best French champagne in the palace of a tribal king. He can experience an unnerving ride over the Congo River rapids in a hand-hewn pirogue—a native dugout —then ten minutes later step aboard a jet plane that will take him to the far corners of the earth.

STRANGE HISTORY

The Congo's past reveals the same unusual pattern of paradox. In the years when barbarian tribes roamed the virgin plains of Europe there was already a mighty, peaceful, well-ruled nation in the Congo basin. It was called the Kingdom of Kongo, and European traders in the sixteenth century offered titles to its African chiefs, who became barons and dukes. Some became Christians, and one went to study theology in Portugal and was made the first Congolese bishop of the Catholic Church by Pope Leo X in 1520. Congolese emissaries were sent to the Vatican for several centuries, and the country had considerable status. These early Congolese had a highly developed society and culture. They knew how to forge and smelt iron, they traded profitably with their neighbors as well as with Europeans, but above all they were masters in their own land.

Then European and Arab slave traders, in their greedy and brutal quest for "black ivory," decimated African populations and demoralized the people. Between them they drained the Congo of a million slaves a year. Some tribes helped to round up and sell their weaker neighbors into captivity, and as a result bitter tribal wars broke out. The feuds that started then have never died out completely. And Europeans, to allay their guilt over the slave traffic, depicted the black man of Africa as a savage fit only for slavery. That image, too, has been a long time dying.

The turning point, both for better and for worse, came in the mid-nineteenth century. For better, public pressures in the United States and Europe brought about the cessation of the slave trade in Africa. Only the Arabs continued it. And Christian missionaries penetrated the equatorial interior, dedicated to the conquest of ignorance, disease and poverty. For worse, those Europeans who profited from exploitation of new lands recognized the potential wealth of equatorial Africa and set about carving up the country into profitable colonies.

EXPLORATION AND EXPLOITATION

A decade before Columbus discovered America while searching for a passage to the Indies, a Portuguese explorer named Diogo Cão (DYOH-*goo* KOWNGH) reached the mouth of the Congo River. He thought the river might cut across Africa to the Indian Ocean, but was hampered in exploring this possible short cut to the Indies by the rapids and falls a hundred miles up the river. The Portuguese built settlements just south of the Congo in what is now Angola (*ahn*-GOH-*lah*).

Europeans did not explore the interior of Africa until the middle of the nineteenth century, when slaving had finally been outlawed. David Livingstone, a Scottish missionary-explorer, discovered the Upper Congo River—which he thought was the Nile—but then he disappeared in the dark heart of Africa. Henry Morton Stanley, a Welsh-born adventurer, was sent by the New York *Herald* to find him. Stanley capped his dramatic mission with the most famous understated line of all time. "Dr.

The historic meeting of Stanley and Livingstone was recorded in this contemporary engraving.

Livingstone, I presume?" was his stately greeting to the white man whom he found encamped near remote Lake Tanganyika (*tan-gan-*YEE-*kah*).

Stanley's Congo explorations fascinated King Leopold II of Belgium, who sent him on a four-year trek to wangle treaties with Congolese chiefs. The Congo Free State was the result of this collaboration, and all 900,000 square miles of it became the personal property of the Belgian king. It was a territory seventy-seven times as large as his own country.

From 1885 to 1908 Leopold's relentless exploitation of the Congo's natural resources and its people earned him a private fortune of mil-

lions of dollars and cost the lives of nearly eight million Congolese.
African workers had their hands or feet cut off if they did not obey their
overseers, and photographic records of these atrocities created international pressures against the cruel regime. As a result, Leopold was
forced to turn the Congo over to the Belgian government.

FIGHT FOR FREEDOM

The wave of nationalism that swept Africa after World War II struck
the Congo in 1957, when riots broke out in Léopoldville (*lay-oh-pold-*
VEEL), its capital. In the previous fifty years Belgium had undoubtedly
accomplished much in the country, but with the exception of town
councils in two small communities, the Congolese were denied the right
to vote and had no voice in the policies by which they were governed.
There were also severe restrictions on higher education, foreign travel
and bearing arms. Such an atmosphere inevitably bred revolution, and
the uprisings culminated in Congolese self-rule in 1960.

The Congo's first year as a republic was torn with strife. Ill-prepared
men grappled for power. Old tribal feuds broke out anew. The rich
Kasai and Katanga provinces tried to secede. Whites were attacked and
missionaries were killed. Prime Minister Patrice Lumumba (*pah-*TREESS
*loo-*MOOM-*bah*) was assassinated, and Katanga leader Moise Tshombe
(*moh-*EEZ *tshohm-*BEH) was imprisoned for a while. United Nations
troops were requested, then resisted, while Communist factions failed
in an attempt to take over the country.

The basic problem was similar to the one that beset the young United
States: Should the Republic of the Congo be a federation of states
under a strong or weak central government? Opposing a strong federal
government were leaders who were jealous of their provincial powers,
and tribal chiefs who rejected threats to their own stern control
over the people. The Belgian owners of the Katanga mines supported
the strife in hopes of preventing confiscation of their heavy investments.
At last, in the summer of 1961, it was generally agreed that there should
indeed be a strong federal government. The country's six provinces
were given representation and the right to impose taxes. There would
probably be some regrouping of tribes within new administrative units,
but until then the six original provinces would stand. Much remained
to be ironed out, but at least the first steps toward country-wide goals
had been taken.

THE PROVINCES OF THE CONGO

The six Congolese provinces have distinct personalities, and each has
a main city with striking characteristics. Léopoldville is the western-

most province, and here we find the twenty-five-mile coastal strip where the Congo empties into the sea. Farther up the river is the nation's capital, also called Léopoldville but nicknamed Léo (LAY-*oh*). This rapidly growing city has a population of 300,000 and the European section even has one skyscraper (called *le Building*), substantial government offices, a fine Museum of African Life, and a university with an atomic reactor. It is at Léopoldville that all Congo River freight must be transferred from boat to railroad, to bypass the miles of cataracts that make the Congo unnavigable below the city.

The busy capital reflects both European and native life, and in contrast to its library, African housing projects, shopping centers and airport, there is a native section of wooden shacks where domestic animals—including tame monkeys—clutter the mud streets, while the beating of Congo drums is heard above the raucous blare of phonograph music.

To the north of Léopoldville is Equator Province. Here the Congo cuts through dense rain forest, and palm oil and rubber are the chief commodities. The city of Coquilhatville (*kaw-kee-yah*-VEEL) has its main street running directly on the equator. Stanley founded the city some eighty years ago, but because of its steamy climate it has never attracted many European settlers.

Easternmost is Eastern Province, and roaming its northeastern highlands are great herds of elephants, once the source of the Congo's ivory wealth. Stanleyville, a picturesque tropical city called Stan (STAHN) for short, is on the river just be-yond Stanley Falls. Its fascinating open-air market is an exotic showcase for African merchandise—masks, spears, wood carvings, vivid batik cloth, and monkey-meat steaks.

The mountains and lakes of Kivu (KEE-*voo*) Province have made it ideal resort country, and many of the Congo's European settlers have chosen to live here. Bukavu (*boo*-KAH-*voo*) is one of the loveliest cities in Africa, built on five fingers of land that reach into Lake

At Elisabethville's modern airport a tribal chieftain stands at ease while Katanga troops line up smartly.

Kivu. A holiday in this region enables the visitor to see the snowy Mountains of the Moon on the Congo-Uganda border, Albert National Park with its exciting African wildlife, and the giant Watusi (*wah-*TOO-*see*), the statuesque tribesmen from neighboring Ruanda-Urundi (*roo-*AHN-*dah-oo-*ROON-*dee*). In Kivu, too, you will find the little people, Pygmies only four feet tall, who roam the Ituri (*ee-*TOOR-*ee*)Forest as their ancestors did centuries ago. These small hunters are believed to be the earliest inhabitants of the Congo.

The two richest provinces of the Republic are Katanga and Kasai, in the southern highlands. Elisabethville, familiarly pronounced *ay-*VEEL, is the prosperous capital of Katanga. Wealth from the copper mines has given its African citizens the highest standard of living on the continent, and they also enjoy one of the pleasantest climates in Africa. Luluabourg (*loo-*LOO-*ah-boor*) is the chief city of diamond-rich Kasai, and it boasts one of the finest museums of African art and folklore.

Strung across the Congo is this strand of sparkling cities, carved out of the jungle by men whose own natures were more stubborn than the Congo's—persistent men who would not be denied their goals. The Congo has always set its own pace, resisting the foreign influences that began centuries ago. But in spite of its resistance, changes have come.

There you have the true personality of the Congo: its rugged majesty attracts the brave, but it surrenders its riches only to the bold. Thus the Congo today remains a unique bridge between the past and the present, poised by the circumstances of its new freedom at the brink of an exciting future.

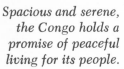

Spacious and serene, the Congo holds a promise of peaceful living for its people.

let's travel in the

CONGO

CONGO RIVERBANK: MAJESTIC WATERWAY

HERE is the vital lifeline of the country—the Congo River. All roads lead to it. The great cities of the land rest on its banks. At any hour of the day, more people travel upon the three-thousand-mile river than on the republic's roads, trains and planes combined. Its vast network of tributaries makes it, in volume, the largest river in Africa, second in the world only to the Amazon, and each day it empties into the Atlantic Ocean three times more water than is used in the same period in the entire United States.

It is a majestic river, a river of many moods. Its distant headwaters sweep across jungle lakes a hundred miles wide, then roar through narrow gorges with scarcely the breadth of a street. At Stanley Falls the Congo plunges down a series of seven cataracts, then curves from north to west, crossing the equator in its course. Its long westerly arc takes it a thousand noble miles, southward at last and across the equator again to Léopoldville. Thus the Congo is the only river in the world to flow in both the Northern and Southern Hemispheres.

Between Léopoldville and Stanleyville no bridge crosses the Congo, no dam bars its path, and the broad river is more like a lake. There are forty thousand islands in the Congo, some of them fifty miles long, and they are resting places for the oarsmen who row their pirogues across the mighty river, which at many places is ten miles wide. A mighty river, yes, but a peaceful one.

Daily the Congolese find many reasons to go down to the riverbank. There may be supplies to unload from barges pushed by stern-wheelers, there may be friends arriving by pirogue from another village, laundry to wash or fish to catch, or simply a free hour for a swim. And there is always the Congo to behold—broad, magnificent, beautiful, bold, mirroring the temperament of the country itself.

16

RAILWAY AT LEOPOLDVILLE: TRACK THROUGH THE JUNGLE

JUST west of Léopoldville a granite barrier a mile wide cuts across the river, holding it back and forcing it to form the broad expanse of water known as Stanley Pool. Below the Pool the river tumbles down a series of cataracts for 215 miles, and this stretch of difficult water prevents vessels from sailing directly to the inland cities from the coast. To provide a supply line from the sea, a railroad has been built from Matadi (*mah-*TAH-*dee*), 85 miles inland at the foot of the falls, to the Léopoldville plateau. Twice a day, wood-burning engines haul long lines of freight cars up the steep hills to the Léopoldville shipyards, and here cargo destined for the interior is loaded aboard the stern-wheelers that ply the Congo River to Stanleyville. Even in the shipyards a slender palm tree and thick baobabs (BAY-*oh-babs*) grow.

Actually, the Matadi-Léopoldville railroad is an unreliable mode of travel. But it is part of the flavor of the Congo that the train should break down several times on its run, that it should stop in the middle of the jungle while the crew chops wood for fuel or that it should stop merely because the engineer has decided to have coffee at the home of a friend who lives nearby. This can be frustrating to an impatient traveler, but it is good that it happens at the start of a Congo visit because there is much more of it ahead.

Native crews man a locomotive—the iron horse now travels through the jungle.

18

CONGOLESE SHOPPING CENTER: LIVELY MARKET PLACE

EVERY weekday morning, two thousand vendors converge on the enormous market in Léopoldville and spread their wares on the ground. Most of them are women and the products they sell are usually homegrown or homemade. Farmers from the surrounding countryside get up in the middle of the night in order to deliver fresh vegetables, chickens and eggs to the market vendors in time for the early morning rush. Cattle and goats are killed in nearby slaughter houses so that the meat will be fresh.

In the course of an average day, easily twenty thousand people come to shop, to browse and to socialize in this noisy supermarket. Above the plaintive cries of the vendors you hear the clamor of arguments over prices or quality, the uncertain groan of dozens of ancient phonographs, the shrieks of lost children, the gruff tones of old men in a political debate, the carefree laughter of young men over their cups of beer. And the market is a kaleidoscope of fascinating scenes. In one corner you might see three boys stamping out a primitive dance while a fourth passes his hat through the audience. Walk on and you are confronted with a buxom matron modeling dazzling dresses, while just ahead a teen-age girl fresh from the bush careens into strangers as she tests her first pair of high-heeled shoes.

The variety of food displayed is amazing: mounds of manioc (a native starch), yams and lima beans, solid walls of bananas, pink hills of sweet tomatoes, tiny gray eggs from scrawny chickens which are also on sale, dried caterpillars, chunks of hippo meat, live fish in buckets, heaps of locusts, skinned monkeys and game birds—the choice is endless and for every taste. In the days before independence, the market was also the forum of the Léopoldville Congolese. It was here that budding political leaders made their first fiery speeches; it was from here that, sadly enough, the first rioters moved out to the European sections of the city. These days the market is again acres of shrill, noisy bargaining.

BALLROOM DANCERS: JAZZ COMES HOME AGAIN

THE sound of a dance band rendering a "pop" song is always a surprise on a quiet Congo evening—the African rhythms have returned in the jazz that they influenced. But to the sophisticated members of the country's youthful elite, ballroom dancing provides a pleasant end to a busy day. Called *évolués (eh-vohl-oo-eh)*—the evolved, the advanced—these young men and women are the new treasures of the Congo. Because of better educations and business skills, they have introduced an important element into Congo life—a middle class. Undoubtedly, their parents back in the tribal villages would have a hard time recognizing them. The idea of a man and a woman embracing in a dance would be unthinkable back home.

In the cities, however, the weekend dance is another indication—a superficial one, to be sure—of the changing attitudes that are slowly releasing the Congo from the rigid customs that for centuries have bound the people to the past and discouraged self-improvement. A significant change, for example, is the new freedom of women. Back home, a girl of marriageable age would not be permitted to have any special boy friend or to go out alone with any man. Her parents would choose her husband, arrange the marriage with his parents, accept the dowry and there she would be, whether she liked her man or not. Thus women were little more than chattels.

Better schools at every level, most of them provided by missionaries, prepared men for better jobs in government, business and the professions, and from this developed the *évolués*. Higher standards of living in cities put greater emphasis on the family than on the tribe. With that, women became more than wives, mothers and housekeepers; they became partners and companions to their husbands, in the home and out of it, and the dance floor is a significant example of their new status.

FISHING
THE RAPIDS:
A QUICK CATCH

THE Congo is a fisherman's paradise, and for the Congolese the paradise is in knowing that the fish are plentiful. Over a thousand different species of fish fill the Congo's lakes and rivers. Using a rod in Lake Albert, you can land a Nile perch weighing a hundred pounds. In the rivers of Kasai Province, a three-hundred-pound nkamba (*n'kahm-bah*) will pull a pirogue full of men ten miles downstream before it gives up the fight.

As much as the bush-country Congolese enjoys sport-fishing, he is primarily interested in getting food for his village. He therefore resorts to techniques that will provide the most fish with the least effort. The most effective method is fishing with traps. Woven from bamboo, these enormous cornucopias range from four to ten feet at the mouth and from ten to fifteen feet in length. The space between the bamboo slats determines the size of fish to be caught. The best trap-fishing is on smaller rivers, particularly where there are rapids, and the traps are held in place by liana vines strung to overhanging trees or to boulders accessible from the shore. The Wagenia (*wah-gheh-nyah*) fishermen, near Stanleyville, are more daring: they build high catwalks over the dangerous rapids of Stanley Falls and shinny out above the seething waters each evening to haul in their fabulous net catches. One misstep would mean death, but the Wagenia consider the prize worth the risk.

In calm waters the spear-fisherman uses this difficult but graceful technique.

INSPECTING THE
FISH TRAPS:
CHILD LABOR

TAKING his place in village life comes early to a Congolese. There is always work to be done and never enough hands to do it. Congolese children of five already have their chores—in the field, in the hut, at the river's edge. To older boys goes the daily task of inspecting the fish traps, repairing them, cleaning them, weaving new traps when the old wear out.

Instead of resenting these restrictions on their playtime, the Congolese youngsters welcome them. To be a working member of their village means that they are growing up, and they are impatient for it. Congo families in the bush are not separated by the necessities of earning a livelihood. During the planting and harvesting seasons, the whole family goes together to the fields to work. When a boy is seven, he joins

Life is fun for an African child. Bath time is simply a cool swim with jolly company.

his father on hunting trips, learning how to track game, how to use a lance and a bow and arrow, how to skin and butcher a gazelle or zebra where it falls. At the same age Congolese girls are taught by their mothers to grind maize, to weave brooms and sleeping mats and to identify the nonpoisonous herbs and wild fruit that fill out the family menu. Being young in the Congo is a time of adventure, discovery and usefulness, certainly a time to be envied by other young people whose chores at home are usually limited to drying dishes or watering the lawn.

VILLAGE CELEBRATION: PARTY TIME

THERE is always time for play in the Congo, always a time when there is something to celebrate with songs and dances. Perhaps the harvest has been especially good or the men have brought back a big supply of meat from their hunt or someone has married or had a baby or is going off on a trip or has just come back. Then work is forgotten. Out come the big drums to provide a rhythmic beat for the dancers and singers; out come the inks and dyes for the women to paint their heads and faces with; out come the beautiful feathers for them to tie to their waistbands. A big fire is built and a goat is prepared for the feast. The party will go on all night—maybe all week.

There are no wallflowers at the village celebration. One group after another gathers around the fire to stomp out an intricate dance, each dance different from the other, each telling the story of some past event of pride or prosperity. With each dance a song is sung, usually a ballad that seems to go on for hours. And why not? The Congolese have a long history, and they keep it alive by dancing and singing its great moments at their fetes.

Gone is the era when songs and dances were also used to incite a village to violence. So stirring, so emotional were such performances that a chief could arouse his people to war by ordering certain dances. Similarly, a witch doctor could assert his power over a village by urging frantic dances intended to appease angry gods. The growth of Christianity has greatly minimized the influence of witch doctors, even upon dancing; the intermixture of various tribes in higher schools has overcome old feuds that once so easily triggered wars. These days, singing and dancing in a Congo village are an indication of a joyous event, and the arrival of a tourist with his camera is excuse enough for a celebration.

WATUSI DANCERS: NEIGHBORING GIANTS

FOR the most colorful and exciting dancing, you must go to Ruanda-Urundi, the Belgian trusteeship east of the Congo. Here the ruling tribe is the Watusi, the tallest people in the world. It has been said that these giants are born six feet tall, and when you walk among them you can believe it. Men towering seven or eight feet are a common sight. Women gain height by having their heads bound into conical shape in infancy, then training their thick hair to grow straight up to add a few inches. Beholding these lean, dignified, soft-spoken giants is quite overwhelming—and they know it.

Legend more than history indicates that the Watusi migrated to the Congo equator some five hundred years ago, probably from the Ethiopian region where there are still other tribes of comparable stature and features. Perhaps war or famine forced the Watusi to leave their home. Reaching the equator, they were able to establish their rule over other tribes by size alone: the Pygmies retreated into the forests, the Batwa became servants of the Watusi. Today they still reign.

When they start dancing, the Watusi discard their usual reserve and become frenzied. Sudden jerks of their heads send their crowns of beaded monkey hair flashing wildly. Twisting, bending, squirming, they leap into the air, breaking high-jump records without missing a beat. They carry spears, and when one jumper soars especially high the others throw down their spears in defeat. But the dance goes on. Ankle bracelets heavy with bells match the earth-trembling thunder of twenty royal drummers. First ten men dance, then fifty, then two hundred, their speed increasing with their number as they fly through intricate routines with thrilling precision and flair. So honored is membership in the royal dance troupe that it is granted by the Mwami (the king) only to the sons of chiefs—and only to the finest of these. The amazing dancers well deserve the regal honors: there is nothing like them in all Africa.

LONGHORN CATTLE: WATUSI STATUS SYMBOLS

THE Watusi cattle are as distinctive as the Watusi dances. You will see these enormous longhorns only on Watusi farms, and the size of the herd indicates both the farmer's wealth and his social position. The Watusi would rather go hungry than butcher their cattle for food. Actually, that precise situation arose a few years ago when big herds required so much pasture land that there was no room to grow vegetables. The Belgian government suggested sending some of the cattle to slaughterhouses but the Watusi refused. Nature finally solved the problem with an epidemic that diminished the herds.

The Watusi brought their cattle along when they migrated to the Congo equator, and today the cattle figure in all important transactions. No matter how much money a man may be willing to pay for new land, he must also pay a few longhorns. Cattle are invariably part of a marriage dowry. And when an honor comes to a man—when he is made a chief or an ordained minister or graduates from a foreign university, his friends give him gifts of cattle. To sell his longhorns without a good reason would be considered scandalous, and the man who did so would be ostracized. Simply by owning a large herd, a man earns the respect of his neighbors and in Watusi country, the status-seeker is not judged on his own merits but by the cattle he keeps.

In big cities like Léopoldville there are other— and less attractive— symbols of affluence.

LITTLE GRASS SCHOOLHOUSE: NATIVE ARCHITECTURE

WHAT could be more African than thatched roofs? And in Africa what could be more practical? In recent years, some well-intentioned Europeans tried to convince the bush-Congolese that they should build themselves more durable homes, but the Europeans soon discovered that the natives had been right in building the way they did. Thatched roofs not only keep a house dry, they keep it cool, and on the equator that is important.

Important, too, is the matter of economy. The elephant grass, the straw and the palm fronds that go into a thatched roof are plentiful and free. When a new house is built, the women collect roofing material from surrounding fields and tie it into thick bunches, then men climb up on the framework and fasten the bunches to bamboo strips. The result is a sturdy roof that will withstand the equatorial downpours and reflect the equatorial sun better than anything else available. Newcomers to the Congo often think the mud huts must be unsanitary places to live, but the opposite is true. The mud walls are baked as solid as brick before the roof is built. The mud floors can be swept as clean as marble. The structure seen here is a classroom of a mission school, with a wall built only on the far side for another practical reason —the rain generally comes from that direction.

These schoolboys are learning to take their place in a world where things must be weighed and measured.

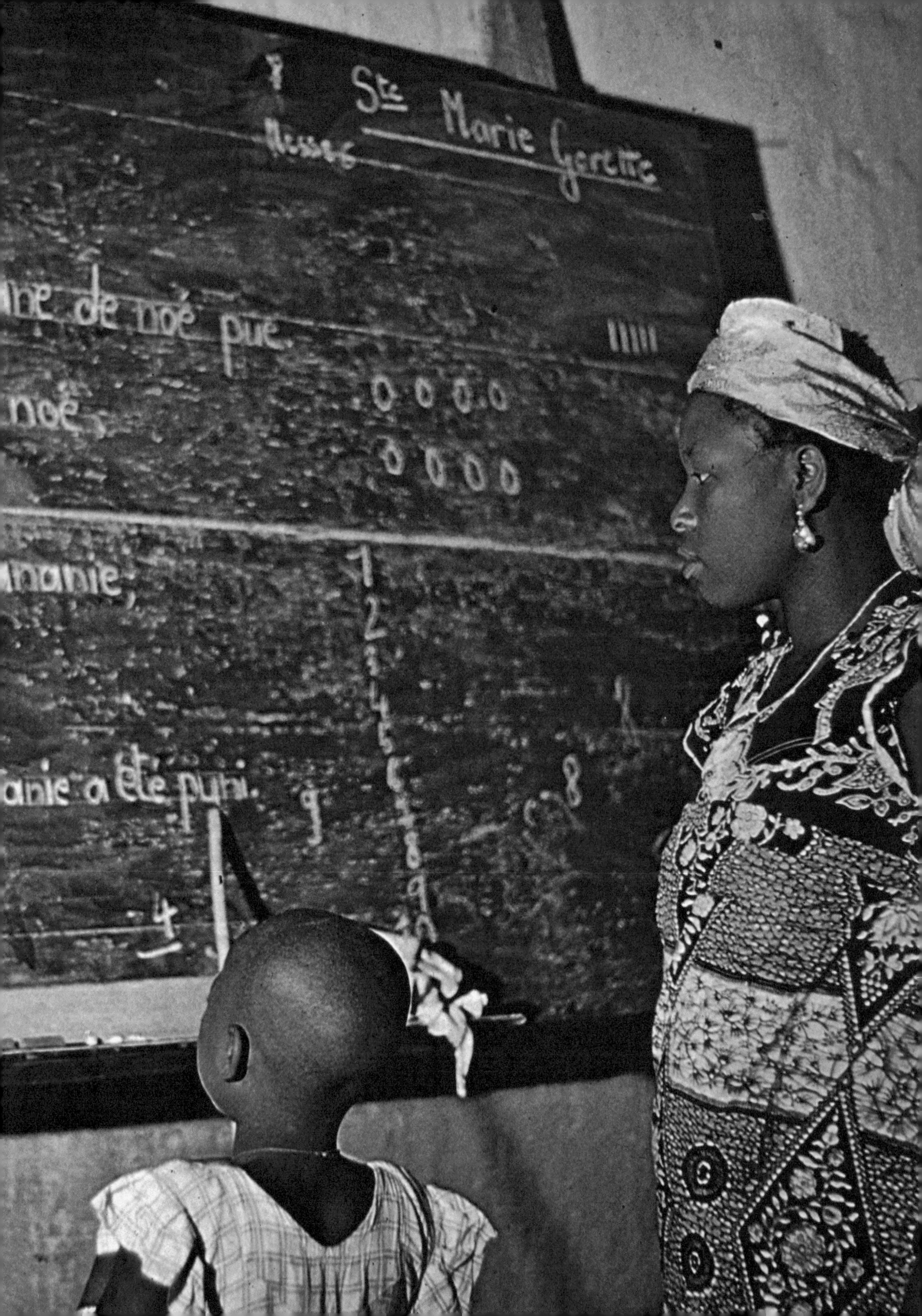
Ste Marie
de noé pue.
noé
a été puni.

NEW EDUCATION:
AFRICA SPEAKS,
READS AND
WRITES

STRANGE as it may seem, Congolese children enjoy school, and one explanation may be that they are not obliged to attend. Even these days, most of them are the first of their family to learn to read and write. Old-timers stubbornly insist that a child can learn at home all he needs to know. But now self-government has put a new emphasis on the importance of education. For the first time, youngsters can look forward to high careers in government, and they realize they must be prepared.

They face a unique problem: language. Each of the Congo's two hundred tribes has its own language; often tribesmen who have been neighbors for years cannot communicate because of the language barrier. Because of the nature of the Congolese school system, a youngster has to become a linguist in the process of being educated. His first two years (primary school) will be in his own village or the nearest mission, so the language will be his own. For the next two years (secondary school), he may have to walk several miles a day to a larger mission where boys of other tribes study with him. Here the school language is usually Kiswahili (KIH-*swah*-HEE-*lee*), an African language that includes Arabic words and is understood by millions of natives, regardless of tribe.

The next four years (middle school) require better textbooks, and these are in the language of the land; in the Congo, this is French. Often a form of "pidgin" French is used to bridge the language gap, but if the boy goes on to high school (senior school) he becomes fluent in French. In college he will use French exclusively—even as a springboard for learning English, German or Spanish, a feat that dispels the old idea that a bush-boy born of illiterate parents cannot be a good student. Congolese exchange students in American universities provide outstanding evidence that, given a chance, they can take their places alongside educated people anywhere in the world.

CUSTOM DRESSMAKERS: HIGH STYLE IN THE BUSH

THIS might well be the Congolese branch of Dior's Parisian salon—and every Congo town has one of them. Lined up along the shady side of every general store are men like these, who earn their living making women's clothes. Their designs may not win any fashion awards, but they would certainly get the prize for quick service. Ten minutes is all it takes for a customer to choose her material from the selection on the line, wrap it around her once to determine the amount she needs, then sit down and wait for the *couturier* to sew on a hem. The price? That depends on the girth of the customer.

But men are customers, too. When he goes off to his job a man may wear shorts or slacks, but at home he dons a sarong-type robe similar to his wife's and for Sundays and holidays he wants one with gaudier prints and bolder colors than hers. A Congolese family dressed to the teeth looks like a walking rainbow.

The Congolese conviction that a woman's place is in the home explains why men do the sewing usually done by women in other lands. Even in the missions and in the homes of Europeans, men servants do the cooking and the housework. Men are nurses in the hospitals, clerks in the shops and typists in the offices. Such jobs enable men to earn extra money while their wives remain home, raising the children, weeding the vegetable garden, attending the cattle. Also, bush-women are still regarded as incapable of doing anything worth being paid for and they are limited to the duties around the house and farm. The growing industrialization of the Congo may change this, but the people aren't sure yet that they will like it.

EASY
LAUGHTER:
A MERRY
PEOPLE

AIM your camera at Congolese women or children and they will erupt in gales of laughter. Being photographed strikes them as the funniest thing in the world, though few of them have actually seen pictures of themselves. But they are delighted that you are paying them so much attention. This is a holiday, and the women are dressed for it. A visit has come to an end. With typical Congolese courtesy, the hostess and her sons have escorted their guests to the crossroads to assure their safety halfway home. Now they will stand there and chat over a long good-bye, as if they were never to see each other again. But chances are they will meet at the market tomorrow, or see each other in the fields or at the mission when they take their babies to see the doctor.

The mission doctor has done a great deal for these women. Just a few years ago, infant mortality was shockingly high because women lacked proper training. Now expectant mothers go to the mission a month before delivery and stay a month after it. Then the baby is taken to the doctor once a week for the first year to make certain all is well. Meanwhile, the mother learns the importance of a balanced diet for her growing children, a rarity in this land where malnutrition is a common ailment. Slowly the old health problems of the Congo are being overcome. Aware of this, the Congolese mothers laugh more easily these days.

Congolese women with children on their laps still manage to keep lessons on their minds.

MARKET DAY IN GOMA: WEEKLY EVENT

APERAMBULATOR for a Congo baby is his mother's back. Whenever she leaves the family hut, she slings her youngest around her back and tucks him firmly inside her robe. Her slow, graceful walk soon lulls the baby to sleep and not even the noise of the market disturbs him. In the smaller towns, market day comes once a week. This one at Goma (GOH-*mah*), on the northern shores of Lake Kivu, is typical of all of them—the same crowds, the same frantic bargaining, the same social occasion to exchange gossip and news.

In this part of the Congo, farms are small. It is the duty of fathers to divide their land among their sons, which means that after a while the pieces will get small indeed. Then the farmer with just an acre or two plants only one crop and depends on it for his livelihood. Around Goma, coffee is the money crop, and the beans grown here find their way into the rich, black brews popular in Germany and Belgium. Some farmers, however, their eyes on market-day profits, cultivate manioc, rice and maize for the coffee-grower's wife when she comes to town with her

Bananas, freshly picked, are carried to market by the farmer. Who needs a middleman?

wicker shopping basket. When she finishes her shopping, Mrs. Coffee-grower will place the basket on her head, walk lithely back to her house, put her baby to bed in a bamboo crib, prepare the dinner and tell her husband all the news she learned that day at the market.

PREPARING DINNER: CHANGELESS MENU

BUSH-COUNTRY Congolese eat only one real meal a day, cooked outdoors in the evening by the mother when her other chores are done. Cold leftovers are sometimes eaten the next morning, or they are wrapped in banana leaves and taken out to the fields for a noon snack. The evening meal seldom varies: bananas, lima beans, manioc, corn mush. If the harvest has been good or the man of the family has a job, there may be tomatoes, sorghum, a piece of goat or a chicken. Despite the abundance of cattle, a cow has too many other values to be used as ordinary table fare unless it has died or is on its last legs.

Except on festive occasions, there is rarely meat unless the men have had some luck hunting. The small fish trap shown in the background of this picture indicates that the woman is better off than many: her meals will include at least some protein, usually a serious shortage in native diets. Improper nutrition makes Africans succumb quickly to diseases, and robs them of the energy to work any more than just enough to survive.

Yet even the *évolués* in big cities seem to prefer the food of their home villages. Undoubtedly, this is the result of habit and time will overcome it. Meanwhile, millions of bush-country Congolese adhere to the centuries-old menus of their forefathers. When you are in the Congo you will want to try the food, preferably in an approved back-country restaurant. You will find that the mashed bananas taste like bitter turnips, that the mush tastes like bland oatmeal, that the palm oil poured over everything tastes like something drained out of your car. You will wonder how anyone manages to exist on it, but that's what the Congolese think of our food the first time they try it.

45

PLATTER-LIPPED BEAUTY: TRIBAL COSMETICS

HERE is certainly a familiar face, though nowadays it is increasingly difficult to find in the Congo. African women first disfigured their faces like this about a hundred years ago, in order to make themselves too ugly for the Arab slave traders to kidnap. After a while their own men got used to the sight and such women began to look good to them. When slavery ended, the alteration was continued as a cosmetic tradition.

The process originated in what was once Ubangi-Shari (*oo*-BAHN-*ghee*-SHAH-*ree*) and is now the Central African Republic. In the Congo it was taken up by the Bunia (BOO-*nyah*) people, in Eastern Province, where older women still go about with platter lips. The younger generation has given it up. It is a painful process, begun in youth by perforating the lips with small sticks, then inserting successively larger discs and finally painting the mouth with a blue dye.

Most Congolese tribes also practice scarification—cutting their faces and bodies with a specific design. Often the wounds are purposely irritated to produce a startling bas-relief of scar tissue. It is probable that scarification was originally used as a form of identification. In the heat of close combat a warrior could quickly recognize his own men by the scars on their faces. Kidnapped children could also be identified by their markings. And if a stranger appeared and said he was a tribesman who had gone away long before, the people had only to examine his markings to see if he was telling the truth. With time the scars have taken on a religious significance. They are thought to ward off evil spirits, and some Congolese who fear spirits more than pain have made their bodies a complete mosaic of scars and tattoos. The women think that proper markings add to their beauty and will often undergo the greatest torture to make themselves more desirable. In this, the Congolese women differ little from their female counterparts around the world.

NATURAL GRACE: AFRICAN WILDLIFE

THE high point of any trip to the Congo is the opportunity to observe its abundance of wild animals. Most of them are surprisingly tame, and you will find that hunting them with your camera is always an exciting and fruitful experience. If you move quietly and calmly, you can approach within a few feet for excellent pictures.

There are four national parks in the Congo, one in the south in Katanga, the others up in the northeast. They are all game reserves where hunting is prohibited; the animals seem to know it, and thus gather there in great numbers. Just seeing the wildlife is enough for most visitors. Young antelope, like this one, are breath-takingly beautiful and graceful to behold. Albert National Park is the world's only reserve for gorillas: you can watch them moving heavily among the low branches at sunset before they settle down for the night.

An always startling sight is the skeleton of some unfortunate creature, like the skull and tusks of an elephant shown here. Whatever the cause of death, vultures, hyenas and ants pick the bones clean within a few hours. Ants are a constant menace, prowling constantly for something to eat and pausing briefly to breed in the tall hills they build. The anthills are formed so quickly that a careless driver may crash into one that wasn't there when he passed that way in the morning.

Pygmy hunters in the jungle surround the mighty giant they have felled.

WORKING ELEPHANTS: INTELLIGENT BEASTS

IT WAS once thought that the African elephant lacked the brains of the Indian elephant and could not be trained to work. But if he is captured before the age of five, the African elephant can be taught to do the heavy draft work around the logging camps and mine fields. Massive yet docile, intelligent and dependable, the magnificent beast is worth many times his weight in human workers.

Untamed Congo elephants usually remain in the woods, and you can see herds of as many as thirty of them grazing on the shores of hidden inland lakes. Unless provoked, they ignore their visitors, and it is not unusual to see a group of travelers enjoying a picnic lunch fifty yards from a herd occupied with its own noon meal. Congo elephants have to eat about seven hundred pounds of food each day to nourish their huge bodies and they also drink about forty gallons of water.

Big as they are, they can be as pesky as insects. Undaunted by man, they will invade a farmer's fields and dig up his potatoes with their tusks. European housewives here yearn for some kind of elephant repellent that will keep the brutes out of vegetable gardens. At harvest time, elephants enter native villages to break into fragile storehouses. They will even go into sizeable towns for a nocturnal eating spree. Next morning, the town is a mess of overturned rubbish cans, raided food trucks and ransacked shops. Bush-country hotels face the same nightly forays.

At the other extreme of the animal kingdom, the Congo has over twenty thousand varieties of insects, but few of them are poisonous. You won't be able to say you've been in the Congo until you have a jigger—a small louse that gets under your toenail. A slight ache tells you it is there, but oddly enough only a native boy is able to see it and dig it out painlessly. He will charge you five cents and you will feel at last like a real world traveler.

50

KING OF THE JUNGLE: LION ON THE PROWL

HERE is the king of Africa —the lion. And a lazy king he is, too. Despite his fierce reputation, he spends most of his time sleeping, and the only time he hunts his own food is when his mate is about to present him with cubs. Lions can run thirty-five miles an hour—usually when they are running away. A lioness, however, is a far different animal. She is the hunter, the killer, and she is also a good wife. After she kills a zebra, gazelle or antelope, she steps aside and lets her husband eat first. On the broad savannas of the eastern Congo, where trees are sparse, you will see prides of lions resting in the shade as they wait for their next meal to trot by.

Ordinarily, only cornered or wounded lions will attack people. However, they can be a real danger if they ever develop a taste for human flesh. Across the border in Tanganyika, man-eaters once killed five hundred Africans in a single year. It is the lion's roar that accounts for most of the fear people have for him. At night he can be heard seven miles away, but usually he is merely looking for a mate. When he becomes a father, the lion behaves like a family man and hunts down small animals for his mate and cubs, but he grows bored easily and may eat his cubs if he thinks they are holding him down. Even so, he is a majestic animal to watch as he lopes across a field—a noble king whose crown is protected by his wife.

A swarm of locusts can prove more trouble than the large, fierce African game.

MASKED DANCER: EVIL SPIRITS, BEWARE!

THERE are spirits loose in the land, evil spirits that can wither a man's crops, dry up his cows and make his wife barren. The spirits must be appeased or they may set fire to a man's house or send pestilence to his village. Such is the belief of the Mingangi (*meen-*GAHN-*ghee*) people of the central Congo. In appeasement, they don brilliant costumes and terrifying masks to dance frantically around enormous fires.

Of all the Congo tribes, the Mingangi people have been the most difficult to civilize. Cut off from the world by the jungle, they have clung rigidly to their old ways. Many of them were converted to Mohammedanism by the Arab slave traders, but still they adhere to their pagan tenets. They will tell you that they became Moslems to win favor with the traders, who then paid them to kidnap other Congolese, and they still prefer Islam to Christianity because it allows them to continue their polygamy. The Arabs also imbued the tribes with an abiding hatred of whites. These were the people who so quickly responded to the battle cry against Europeans during the uprisings, rampaging out of the forests to behead missionaries, burn the homes of settlers and steal cattle.

In normal times, the Mingangi people live quietly in their primitive villages deep in the jungle. Because of their inaccessibility they receive few visitors, but if you arrive when they are about to practice their religious rites they will let you stay for a while and photograph them. It might be better, however, to be on your way before the ceremonies reach full pitch. Often the rituals include sacrifices, and although the Mingangi people will deny it now, it is well known that they used to be cannibals.

PAGAN RITES: FANTASTIC MASQUERADE

SOON the drums will begin and these three men will come forward to start their Mingangi dance. Twisting, turning, leaping, they present a startling scene of bizarre beauty. But beauty is not their purpose: their grotesque costumes are supposed to make them look like the evil spirits they fear, and if they can make themselves look even more fearsome, the spirits may go away.

African paganism differs little anywhere on the continent. The people believe in God, but they believe that between Him and mankind is a universe of good and evil spirits that compete to rule the lives of men. On death, everybody enters this universe, thereafter to affect the living in some way. Thus, when a man has a streak of bad luck, he will find out whether a personal enemy has died. If so, he will try to make peace by sacrifices, by doing something helpful for his enemy's relatives or by paying the witch doctor to remove any curse put upon him. In the same way, good luck means a friendly spirit is abroad, and a man will resort to similar means to show his gratitude.

But the evil spirits are the busier. If one night on a lonely road an owl hoots in a certain tree or bats soar out of an abandoned house, a frightened man will never walk that path again: an evil spirit is there. Anything unusual or unexpected is regarded with the same suspicion. A woman who has twins has surely been cursed: she must kill one of them, sometimes both. Sickness, sudden death, unfavorable weather— all are curses. On the other hand, the good spirit of a handsome prince is supposed to live in the body of every pied wagtail, the beautiful bird of Ruanda, and if the bird lights on your doorstep you will have a happy marriage. The witch doctor can arrange this for you merely by sprinkling seeds at your door, but a good pagan believes the bird arrives on its own.

CONGO DRUMS: SYNCOPATED BEAT

THE first time you hear the drums of the Congo you feel that you are really in Africa at last. Their rhythmic thunder at dawn on a feast day sends you leaping from your bed in stunned wonder. Here is the Congo as you expected it to be. The Congolese love their drums, too. These children at a school near Elisabethville are already skilled players. Each drum has its own sound, and an ensemble of them produces as many tones as an orchestra. Even at this age the youngsters know the blends and beats that start the feet stamping and the hands clapping. Once turned loose, the boys and girls are willing to play all day—and usually do.

For subtler music the Congolese have a wide range of instruments, but drums remain their favorite. In many places, drums are still used to transmit messages. Recently a recording company sent engineers to a village in the Congo to tape the traditional drum messages. The players worked their way through every rhythm in their repertoire, finally reaching the long and somber announcement of a death. After an hour of it, an old man staggered from the bush, tears streaming down his face, sobs racking his body. He stopped in front of the drummers and wailed, "Who died?"

Popular music— owes its insistent beat to the songs that came out of Africa.

MODERN COMPANY TOWN: KATANGA PROVINCE

INDUSTRY, which the Congo needs badly, makes its mark upon a country. At the present time, the biggest industry in the Congo is mining, most of it in Katanga Province. And this is mining on an enormous scale. Seven per cent of the world's copper, 80 per cent of the cobalt and 5 per cent of the zinc come from Katanga. The uranium that went into the world's first atomic bomb also came from here.

Katanga accounts for almost half of the Congo's exports and pays half of the country's taxes. A skilled mine worker can earn a hundred dollars a month, the highest salary for labor in Africa. For over a century, the Congo's mines were owned principally by the Belgian government and labor had to be conscripted from distant tribes. In recent years, however, every effort was made to attract volunteer workers, with the result that Katanga offers the highest standard of living on the equator.

Free housing has been provided in villages like the one shown here, where electricity and running water were recently installed. Now a man can live with his wife and children when he works in the mines; in the past, he came alone for two or three years—a great threat to family unity. The villages also have good schools and hospitals, and the law is kept by fez-wearing police like the ones in this picture. Even food and clothing are provided free.

The amazing profits from mining have made these benefits worthwhile to the Belgian operators. When self-government was granted, the Belgians expected to hold on to their Katanga interests, but then the late Premier Patrice Lumumba ordered all Belgians out of the country. Stunned, the operators quickly got behind Moise Tshombe, a wealthy chief who opposed Lumumba, and Tshombe promptly announced that Katanga was seceding from the Republic. Now a compromise has been reached, assuring the future of the mining villages and offering the hope that other industries may follow suit and provide workers with modern necessities they cannot yet afford on their own.

DIAMONDS IN
THE EARTH:
KASAI
TREASURE-TROVE

IN THE heart of the scrawny scrublands of Kasai Province lies one of the great treasures of Africa—rich mines that produce most of the world's industrial diamonds. The stones are small, averaging one carat in weight, but they are of the best quality and bring high prices on the London market.

Unlike the Tanganyika and South African diamonds, which are buried deep in the ground, the Kasai stones are found in gravel strata ranging from three to twenty feet below the surface. When a strike is located, cranes move in and shovel the gravel into dump trucks. The precious cargo is then hauled by rail to the concentrators, where it is washed.

This Congolese belle prefers a fiber comb and shell beads to the diamonds that are mined in the country.

Then it is poured on inclined tables treated with a special grease that holds the diamonds but lets the gravel slide away. Each day cartons of rough diamonds are flown to London to be polished and cut, eventually finding their way to factories around the world.

Once a strike is drained, the long crevasse is flooded with waters from the Lubilash (*loo*-BEE-*lash*) River, beginning again the long process which may produce another sparkling treasury in another million years.

VOLCANIC LANDSCAPE: EQUATORIAL WASTELAND

THIS is the eerie lava road on the northern shores of Lake Kivu. Not far from here are the fabled Mountains of the Moon, snow-capped peaks where icy summits rise almost directly above the equator. There are three active volcanoes in this region, and the one called Nyamlagira (*nyahm-lah-*GHEE-*rah*) erupted in 1938, sending a six-mile-wide sheet of lava twenty miles to the lake and cutting off the road to Sake (*sah-keh.*) Two years passed before the lava cooled and hardened. From habit, the people resumed driving over it—and the lava road was born.

Strangely, the most beautiful part of the Congo adjoins this broad devastation. Many travelers consider Lake Kivu lovelier than the lakes of Italy. Along the shore road at Goma are rows of summer mansions, and at Kisenyi (*kee-*SEN-*yee*), across the border in Ruanda, are elegant hotels for tourists. The fifty-mile lake lies like a jewel in the verdant foothills. Because of its elevation—five thousand feet—there is no malaria. It is the only sizeable lake on the equator that is free of crocodiles and hippopotamuses. The waters of Lake Tanganyika, just a hundred miles away, are alive with more than 3,000,000 crocodiles. And because of the volcanic ash that has fallen into Lake Kivu over the centuries, there are none of the infected snails that can cause a blinding disease in all other large bodies of water in Africa.

Here is the heart of the Congo vacationland. In addition to having your pick of the finest accommodations available anywhere, you are just a short drive from the Ituri Forest, where the Pygmies live. Go on a few miles over the Kabasha (*kah-*BAH-*shah*) Escarpment and you are in Albert National Park, the protected home of the increasingly rare gorillas. Or leave your hotel after breakfast and drive east in time to watch the magnificent Watusi dancers before lunch. Excursion boats on the lake can take you down to Bukavu to shops as fine as any in Rome, to restaurants that equal the best in Paris. This is the part of the Congo you may remember longest because it is the part you didn't expect.

ARTISTIC WARRIORS: THE BRUSH IS MIGHTIER THAN THE SPEAR

PROBABLY the most artistic of the Congo tribes are the Mangbetu (*mahng*-BEH-*too*), who live in the northern Congo along the Sudan border. A blank wall challenges them. They cannot rest until they have covered it with their intricate designs, masterful work that surely represents primitive art in its highest form. Aquatic figures are their favorites, as is evident in the fish and crocodile on the wall behind these warriors. When we look at this striking mural we are reminded that modern art of the twentieth century owes a great debt to the traditional arts of old Africa.

An unusually advanced tribe, the Mangbetu are the only people known to have made their own furniture before it was introduced by the Arabs and Europeans, a characteristic that indicates contact with some other civilization, perhaps along the Nile River or the Mediterranean shores.

The stately Mangbetu women are works of art in themselves. They

Pure African art has strength and nobility, but under European influence it becomes oddly awkward.

wear only a skirt, which includes a highly decorated bamboo shield in the back that serves as a chair when they sit down. The Mangbetu warriors, who appear formidable at first sight, actually discarded their ferocity years ago. They occupy themselves these days with agriculture—when they can take time off from their painting.

66

SOLEMN CEREMONY: A YOUTH COMES OF AGE

THE young man kneels before the witch doctor for this, the most solemn moment of his life. He is a man now, ready to take his place among other men of his tribe. This is his coming-of-age ceremony.

Maturity is defined in various ways by different tribes. To prove his manliness in advance, a youth may have to kill a lion by himself. Or he may have to bring in a crocodile on his own, or make the first daring assault upon an elephant. In some tribes, he may be sent into the jungle alone, to fend for himself for a month. Whatever the requirement, if he fails he will forever remain a boy in the minds of his clansmen, forbidden to marry, forbidden to take part in the affairs of men.

Once manhood is proved, the youth and others of his age group who have qualified are taken away from the village for a few days of counseling by the tribal elders. Now they are told whatever facts of life they may not already know. They are taught the laws of the tribe and warned that if, as men, they break the laws, they must accept the punishment of men, which can be death. They learn, too, the taboos of the tribe, the severe restrictions that will govern their future conduct towards all others.

Now comes the big day: the youths are brought back to the village. A feast has been prepared. Soon there will be dancing and singing and the drums will beat all night. But first the actual ceremony. Each youth approaches the witch doctor, kneels before him and takes the oath of obedience to the chief and loyalty to the tribe, and then he is circumcised. If he shows the slightest awareness of pain, he is ostracized.

The crowd waits. None of the youthful faces indicates any discomfort. They are truly all men. Let the celebration begin!

CONGOLESE WAR DANCE: FEROCIOUS PAST

THE days are gone now when warriors like these were the terror of the Congo. Today they pick up their spear and shield only when they are on their way to the dance field to act out the victories won by warriors of the past. There was a time, however, not long ago, when tribal wars were the main occupation of all able-bodied men, and the more ferocious they could make themselves look, the more confident they were of success.

In Congolese wars, personal appearance was a psychological weapon. The sight of hundreds of men running across an open field behind a wall of dazzling shields was enough to unnerve even the most determined enemy. Headpieces of flowers and feathers plus a waistband of leaves provided such perfect camouflage in the thick jungle that the enemy had no idea how many men were advancing against him until it was too late.

These were brutal wars. The weapons of spears and knives required infighting, and rare indeed was the man whose body did not bear the scars of battle, whether his side had won or lost. Men fought because their tribes needed more land, because some affront had been committed against them, or to avenge a robbery or a kidnaping. And they fought, sadly enough, out of old feuds that had long since lost their meaning and importance. When self-rule was granted, some Europeans feared the old jealousies would flare up and tribal wars would once again flame across the land. Some skirmishes did break out in Kasai Province, where the Baluba tribe sought to assert its dominance. But that tribal conflict remained a local one, and it was hopeful evidence for peace in the Republic.

TATTOOED DANCER: HALLMARK OF PRIDE

HOW proud he is, this Topoké (*toh-poh-*KEH) dancer! With his head thrown back, he struts the tale of his glorious heritage. The tattoo on his chest and arms is the mark of the man: he considers himself something to show off. And he is indeed to be admired, if only for the pain he willingly endured to have his body etched until it looks like a Persian rug. The design is more than art: it identifies the man. No matter how far he wanders from his village on the Congo River near Stanleyville, he has only to bare his chest to let strangers know that he is a Topoké, a man to be reckoned with.

The only Congolese who need no identifying marks are the Pygmies. Their small stature is their identity. Mature Pygmy men stand under five feet tall, and their poverty also marks them. Primarily hunters, they live on the small game they catch in the Ituri Forest. Efforts have been made to interest the Pygmies in agriculture so they can raise a money crop, but they are nomads who wandered in times past as far as the Mediterranean. There the ancient Greeks first saw them and named them for a Greek measure of length, the distance from elbow to knuckles. With time, the Pygmies have outgrown their suspicion of strangers and it is possible now to enter their temporary villages without danger, but they still prefer to wander freely in the dense forests, unchanged from what they have been since time began.

This little boy, as yet unmarked, stares in awe at the rich design carved on a mask.

HYPNOTIC SPELL: WITCH DOCTOR'S MAGIC

FEW people have held so tight a grip on the Congo for so long as the witch doctors. Their principal tools are fear and ignorance, and they use them cleverly, shrewdly, viciously. The more primitive the tribe, the more powerful the witch doctor, and yet even the most enlightened urban Congolese still harbors a certain terrified respect for witchcraft. The witch doctor has a hypnotic power over his people, sometimes so intense that under this influence a man can pierce his cheeks with arrows and suffer no pain or bleeding. Seeing this, others believe that the witch doctor is omnipotent. Thus it is often he who decides the village's stand on national issues, and invariably he will choose the side that threatens his position the least. He is always against education, hospitals, court justice, political rights—anything that may free his people from his spell.

It is powerful magic. When the witch doctor dons his crown of parrot feathers, when he hangs gourds of weird potions around his neck, when he wails his chant and throws his assortment of colored stones and bone chips on the ground to read the messages of the spirits, he becomes an awesome figure, overwhelming enough to incite his people to riot and murder. In some areas the number of witch doctors has decreased, but those who remain still bind their people with chains of ancient evils.

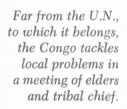

Far from the U.N., to which it belongs, the Congo tackles local problems in a meeting of elders and tribal chief.

AFRICAN CHRISTIANITY: A NEW WAY OF LIFE

THERE is another spiritual force in the Congo, undoubtedly the most vital agency for good in the country: the missions. Because of them the Congo has more primary schools than any other African country, a higher literacy rate, more skilled workers, better hospitals, broader opportunities for self-improvement.

Still more important have been the new ideas which Christianity has introduced into Congolese life. Before the missionaries arrived, Congo languages had no words for brotherhood, charity, forgiveness, renunciation, justice, duty. These were emotions the Congolese did not feel. Over the past hundred years, Protestant and Catholic missionaries have gone to the Congo from all over the Western world. These men and women frequently sacrificed their lives to bring a new life to the Congolese. They knew that hospitals and schools were essential, but they also believed that progress would be an empty thing without spiritual development.

In numbers, the growth of Christianity in Africa appears to be slow. After a century, only 33,000,000 of Africa's 225,000,000 souls are Christians. Almost three times as many are Moslems, but their religion is rife with paganism, and the remainder are utter pagans. Even so, it is Christianity that has made the most positive impression.

As you drive through the Congo, you can tell you are approaching a mission long before you see it. There is a sudden neatness to the land, crops are better, homes are sturdier, the people are better dressed and they appear happier. The heavy air of lethargy that permeates so much of Africa is not felt here. Here there seems to be more purpose, more direction, more meaning to life. You hear it when young men tell you their hopes and plans for their new country, you see it when you watch a woman pause a moment to pray at a wayside shrine.

FUTURE CITIZENS
OF THE WORLD:
BRIGHT-EYED
CHILDREN

THE future of any country lies with its young people, and this is especially true of the Congo. The youth of this country today will be its first generation to grow up with the promise of freedom and justice for all. There will be growing pains, as there have always been in new lands. A nation, like a child, must learn to walk before it can run. A people, despite the many differences among them, must learn to trust in order to become trustworthy.

The Congo offers visitors many wonders to behold—mighty rivers, majestic waterfalls, dense forests, a wealth of natural resources, fascinating animal life, great cities, delightful back-country villages. But nothing is more wondrous than these, its children. On their first day at school, they are beginning the long road that can take them to positions of honor and leadership among all men. Evidence of this vital beginning is apparent everywhere in the country, and it makes a visit to the Congo more than a vacation. It is an adventure in living history.

A statue of a Congolese tribesman seems about to step over the threshold into a bright new world.

SOME FAMOUS NAMES IN CONGO HISTORY

PTOLEMY (2nd century A.D.)—*Greco-Egyptian geographer who sketched first map of Congo interior, based on observations of pioneer explorers.*

DIOGO CAO (15th century)—*Portuguese explorer. Discovered the mouth of the Congo River in 1484 and claimed the area in the name of King John II.*

KING ALVERES I (15th century)—*Ruler of the Kingdom of the Kongo who welcomed Portuguese interests, became a Christian and established diplomatic relations with Portugal, Spain and Rome.*

BISHOP ENRIQUE (16th century)—*Son of King Garcia Alfonse II of Kongo. Studied theology in Portugal and in 1520 became the first Congolese bishop in history.*

DAVID LIVINGSTONE (1813-1873)—*Scottish Protestant missionary. For over thirty years he explored Equatorial Africa, the first white man to see much of it. Due to his efforts, the first steps were taken to end slave trading.*

HENRY MORTON STANLEY (1841-1904)—*Welsh-born American newspaperman; real name, John Rowlands. Assigned by the New York* Herald *to find Livingstone, who was missing in Tanganyika. Later he made extensive trips through the Congo.*

KING LEOPOLD II (1835-1909)—*Ruler of Belgium. As an outcome of founding the International African Association, he became sole owner of the entire Congo and hired Stanley to explore it and make treaties with tribal leaders. His cruel exploitation stirred great public hostility, forcing him to surrender his ownership.*

TIPOO TIB (1837?-1905)—*A rich Arab merchant, he was strong-arm ruler in the eastern Congo and conducted slavery transactions. Surrendering to Stanley, he provided troops for further explorations that led to discovering the sources of the Congo River.*

CARDINAL CHARLES LAVIGERIE (1825-1892)—*French Roman Catholic prelate. Before becoming Archbishop of Algiers, he spearheaded anti-slavery programs which resulted in official abolition. Later he founded the White Fathers, who built the first schools and hospitals in Eastern Congo.*

KING BAUDOUIN (1930-   )—*Belgian ruler who in 1959 announced the granting of self-government to the Congo.*

JOSEPH KASAVUBU (1917-   )—*First president of the Republic of the Congo.*

PATRICE LUMUMBA (1926-1961)—*First prime minister of the Congo, he was assassinated after a brief and stormy career.*

JOSEPH MOBUTU (1930-   )—*Congolese army officer who took over command of the Congo early in its recent violence, subsequently returning control to Kasavubu.*

MOISE TSHOMBE (1919-   )—*Wealthy Katanga Province leader who opposed federation to the point of threatening the entire country. He was removed from office by Mobutu troops but later returned.*

ANTOINE GIZENGA (1920-   )—*Leader of Eastern Province with headquarters in Stanleyville. His Communist-backed regime advocated secession of Eastern Province from the Congo.*

SOME FAMOUS DATES IN CONGO HISTORY

Prehistoric Age — *Evidence of pre-human species of the pygmoid races, found in the northeast and southeast of the Congo, has given substance to the belief that the Pygmies are the original human population of the country.*

Pre-Christian Era — *As early as 5000 B.C., an average-sized people apparently begins migrating into the Congo from Atlantic coast and sub-Sahara regions. In 550 B.C., Phoenician ships circumnavigate Africa and report seeing an enormous river, presumably the Congo, on the west coast. By 200 B.C., the Egyptians know of the great lakes at the equator.*

2nd century A.D. — *Ptolemy produces his map of the Congo interior.*

750 — *Arab caravans reach the Congo area from the east, building forts along their route.*

1484 — *Diogo Cão discovers the mouth of the Congo River. The Kingdom of the Kongo exists at this time. The Watusi have settled in Ruanda.*

1582 — *Missionaries reach Stanley Pool.*

1830 — *Arab slave-trading is accelerated in eastern Congo.*

1857 — *Major Richard Burton and Captain John Speke discover the great lakes and the source of the White Nile. Later, Samuel Baker finds the source of the Blue Nile in the Congo.*

1866 — *Livingstone enters the Congo from the east on his third journey to Africa.*

1871 — *Stanley finds Livingstone on the shore of Lake Tanganyika. Livingstone refuses to leave Africa and dies there in 1873.*

1876 — *Stanley crosses the Congo from the east. King Leopold founds the International African Association and hires Stanley to return to the Congo.*

1885 — *The Belgian Conference awards the Congo to Leopold. The Congo Free State is established.*

1908 — *Public resentment against cruelties in the Congo forces Leopold to surrender personal ownership. The Congo becomes a Belgian colony.*

1919 — *Ruanda-Urundi, made German territory at the Berlin Conference, is turned over to Belgium under a League of Nations mandate.*

1960 — *The Republic of the Congo is established on June 30.*

SOME KISWAHILI WORDS AND PHRASES

There is a great confusion of native languages in the Congo—some are spoken by only a handful of people. In the cities, French is spoken by all the business people you will encounter, and many of them also know English. In the bush, especially in the east where most tourist attractions are, it is good to know some Kiswahili, for it is the common language of millions of Africans in that region.

Do you speak English?	Unasema Kiingereza? (*oo-nah-*SEH-*mah keen-geh* REH-*zah*)
Can you help me?	Unaweza kunisa idia? (*oo-nah-*WEH-*sah koo-nee-sah yee-*DEE-*ah*)
I want a guide who speaks English.	Nataka mwongozi mwenye kusema Kiingereza (*nah-*TAH-*kah em-wohn-*GOH-*zee em-*WEHN-*yay koo-*SEH-*mah keen-geh-*REH-*zah*)
Yes. No. Perhaps.	Ndiyo (*en-*DEE-*yoh*) Hapana (*hah-*PAH-*nah*) Labda (LAHB-*dah*)
Thanks (very much).	Asante (sana) *ah-*SAHN-*tay* (SAH-*nah*)
Please.	Tafadhali (*tah-fahd-*HAH-*lee*)
Excuse me.	Pole (POH-*lay*)
What do you wish?	Unataka nini? (*oo-nah-*TAH-*kah* NEE-*nee*)
Why? When?	Kwa nini? (KWAH NEE-*nee*) Lini? (LEE-*nee*)
Who? What?	Nani? (NAH-*nee*) Nini? (NEE-*nee*)
How? How long?	Namna gani? (NAM-*nah* GAH-*nee*) Mpaka lini? (*m'*PAH-*kah* LEE-*nee*)
Where is . . . ?	. . . ni wapi? (*nee* WAH-*pee*)
Ladies' room	Choo cha wanawake (CHOH-*oh chah wah-nah-*WAH-*keh*)
Men's room	Choo cha wanaume (CHOH-*oh chah wah-na-oo-meh*)
Airport	Kiwanja cha ndge (*kee-*WAHN-*jah chah en-*DEE-*gee*)
Bus station	Kiwanja cha bus (*kee-*WAHN-*jah chah boos*)
Railroad station	Stesheni (*steh-*SHEH-*nee*)
DAYS OF THE WEEK	Siku za Juma (SEE-*koo zah* JOO-*mah*)
Monday	Juma tatu (JOO-*mah* TAH-*tu*)
Tuesday	Juma nne (JOO-*mah* N'*neh*)
Wednesday	Juma tano (JOO-*mah* TAH-*noh*)
Thursday	Alhamisi (*el hah-*MEE-*see*)
Friday	Ijumaa (*ee-joo-*MAH-*ah*)
Saturday	Juma Mosi (JOO-*mah* MOH-*si*)
Sunday	Siku ya Mungu (SEE-*koo yah* MOON-*goo*)
Day Night	Mchana (*m'* CHAH-*nah*) Ussiku (*oo-*SEE-*koo*)
Yesterday Tomorrow	Jana (JAH-*nah*) Kesho (KEH-*shoh*)
Today Tonight	Leo (LEH-*oh*) Leo Ussiku (LEH-*oh oo-*SEE-*koo*)
NUMBERS	Hesabu (*heh-*SAH-*boo*)
One	Moja (MOH-*jah*)
Two	Mbili (*m'*BEE-*lee*)
Three	Tatu (TAH-*too*)
Four	Nne (N'*neh*)
Five	Tano (TAH-*noh*)
Six	Sita (SEE-*tah*)
Seven	Saba (*SAH-*bah*)
Eight	Nane (NAH-*neh*)
Nine	Tisa (*TEE-*sah*)
Ten	Kumi (KOO-*mee*)
One hundred	Mia (MEE-*ah*)
One thousand	Elfu (EL-*foo*)
MONEY	Pesa (PEH-*sah*)
Franc	Franci (FRAHN-*kee*)

INDEX